Fast
Animals

THIS EDITION
Editorial Management by Oriel Square
Produced for DK by WonderLab Group LLC
Jennifer Emmett, Erica Green, Kate Hale, *Founders*

Editors Grace Hill Smith, Libby Romero, Maya Myers, Michaela Weglinski;
Photography Editors Kelley Miller, Annette Kiesow, Nicole DiMella;
Managing Editor Rachel Houghton; **Designers** Project Design Company;
Researcher Michelle Harris; **Copy Editor** Lori Merritt; **Indexer** Connie Binder; **Proofreader** Larry Shea;
Reading Specialist Dr. Jennifer Albro; **Curriculum Specialist** Elaine Larson

Published in the United States by DK Publishing
1745 Broadway, 20th Floor, New York, NY 10019

Copyright © 2023 Dorling Kindersley Limited
DK, a Division of Penguin Random House LLC
23 24 25 26 10 9 8 7 6 5 4 3 2 1
001–334126–Sept/2023

All rights reserved.

Without limiting the rights under the copyright reserved above, no part of this publication may be reproduced, stored in or introduced into a retrieval system, or transmitted, in any form, or by any means (electronic, mechanical, photocopying, recording, or otherwise), without the prior written permission of the copyright owner.
Published in Great Britain by Dorling Kindersley Limited

A catalog record for this book
is available from the Library of Congress.
HC ISBN: 978-0-7440-7570-0
PB ISBN: 978-0-7440-7571-7

DK books are available at special discounts when purchased in bulk for sales promotions, premiums, fundraising, or educational use. For details, contact: DK Publishing Special Markets,
1745 Broadway, 20th Floor, New York, NY 10019
SpecialSales@dk.com

Printed and bound in China

The publisher would like to thank the following for their kind permission to reproduce their images:
a=above; c=center; b=below; l=left; r=right; t=top; b/g=background

123RF.com: Eric Isselee / isselee 19bl, smileus 25bl; **Alamy Stock Photo:** Rick & Nora Bowers 27bl, Dominique Braud / Dembinsky Photo Associates 6-7, Michael Patrick O'Neill 5br, Kevin Schafer 11br; **BluePlanetArchive.com:** Michael Patrick O'Neill 10-11; **Dreamstime.com:** Adwo 1b, John Anderson 31clb, Rinus Baak 18br, 31cl, Natalia Bachkova 31cla, Bryan Busovicki 29bl, Harry Collins 23cr, Donyanedomam 8-9, 9bl, Ecophoto 16bc, Natalia Golovina 16-17, Ken Griffiths 22-23, 23bl, Japonikus 14br, 15b, Roger Johansen 5tr, Cathy Keifer / Cathykeifer 18-19, Matthijs Kuijpers 12cb, Mikael Males 7br, 31bl, Jan Pokorn / Pokec 25br, Stu Porter 4-5, 28br, 29tr, 29br, Slowmotiongli 17bl, John Stocker 6cb; **Getty Images:** imageBROKER / Jurgen & Christine Sohns 24-25, The Image Bank / Winfried Wisniewski 3cb, 30; **Getty Images / iStock:** E+ / Freder 28-29, Thierry Eindeweil 20-21, Edward Palm 14-15, the4js 26br; **naturepl.com:** Karine Aigner 26-27, Juergen Freund 11bl; **Shutterstock.com:** Gerald Robert Fischer 21bc, NickEvansKZN 13br, Cormac Price 12-13, Ferdy Timmerman 31tl, Brian A Wolf 7bl

Cover images: *Front:* **Dreamstime.com:** Martin Malchev, Anastasia Maslova cl; **Getty Images / iStock:** Godruma b;
Back: **Dreamstime.com:** Yayamayka cra

All other images © Dorling Kindersley
For more information see: www.dkimages.com

For the curious
www.dk.com

Fast
Animals

Ruth A. Musgrave

Animals run, fly, and swim.
Let's race to find fast animals.

This baby runs fast.
It runs faster than
a child.

pronghorn antelope

This bird flaps its wings fast.
Can you see its wings?

broad-tailed hummingbird

This turtle swims fast.
Big fish want
to eat it.
It swims fast
to get away.

leatherback sea turtle

Other animals want
to eat this snake.
It moves fast
to get away.
It moves as fast as
a person riding a bike.

black mamba

dragonfly

This bug flies fast
to catch its food.
It grabs other bugs
from the air.

This bird cannot fly.
It runs fast.
It takes big steps.
One step is as long as a car.

ostrich

17

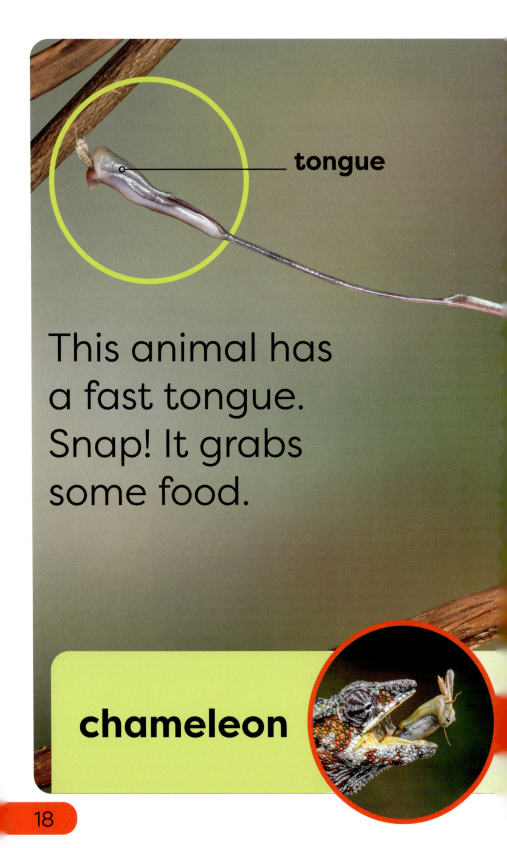

tongue

This animal has a fast tongue. Snap! It grabs some food.

chameleon

This shrimp has fast claws. It uses them to catch food.

peacock mantis shrimp

21

This bird dives fast. It is the fastest diver. It catches other birds in the air.

peregrine falcon

23

Hop, hop.
This animal hops fast.
It has big feet
and strong legs.

kangaroo

This bat flies fast.
It races through
the air.
It catches bugs
to eat.

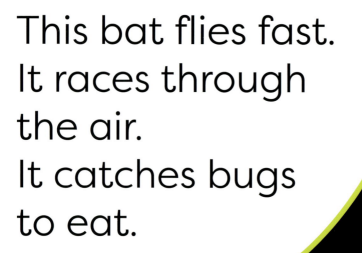

free-tailed bat

This cat runs fast.
It is the fastest runner on land.
It races to catch its food.

cheetah

Fast animals are everywhere.
They move fast to find food or to stay safe.
Which one would you like to be?

Glossary

chameleon
a reptile that lives in trees

dragonfly
an insect that lives near water and has four wings

hummingbird
a fast bird that drinks nectar from flowers

mantis shrimp
an ocean animal that hides in the sand

pronghorn antelope
an animal with hooves that lives in the grasslands

Quiz

Answer the questions to see what you've learned. Check your answers with an adult.

1. What kind of baby runs faster than you?
2. What bug catches other bugs from the air?
3. Which bird takes giant steps?
4. Which animal uses its claws to catch food?
5. What is the fastest cat in the world?

1. Pronghorn antelope 2. Dragonfly 3. Ostrich
4. Peacock mantis shrimp 5. Cheetah